Where's Grandma?

Sean Taylor
Illustrated by Jerry Tiritilli

A Harcourt Achieve Imprint

www.Rigby.com
1-800-531-5015

On Saturday, as always, Grandma, Grandpa, and Worrier, their dog, came to collect Frankie in Grandma's little old car.

Frankie's grandma and grandpa were like many grandmas and grandpas. Their hair was white, they wore old-style clothes, and they liked sitting down a lot. But in Frankie's opinion, his grandma and grandpa had a special twinkle in their eyes.

On the way home, they stopped at Mr. Lum's grocery store. Frankie found some flour, sugar, and milk for his grandma.

"What sort of cookies are you going to bake this weekend?" asked Mr. Lum.

"I feel like baking passion fruit cookies," said Grandma.

"That sounds nice," said Mr. Lum, "as long as you know where to find the passion fruits."

"Leave that to me," said Grandma.

The little old car rattled all the way to Grandma and Grandpa's house.

"If I use the rocket boosters, we'll get there quicker," chuckled Grandma.

"Don't you dare!" replied Grandpa. "Those rocket boosters of yours need fixing!"

At the house, Frankie and Grandpa got out, but Grandma stayed in the car.

"I have one more thing to do, but I'll be back in time for milk and cookies at 4:00," she said.

"I'd like to go to your invention shed until Grandma gets back," said Frankie.

"So would I," Grandpa agreed.

Inside Grandpa's shed, there were odds and ends in boxes, things on hooks, and spare parts hanging from the ceiling.

Grandpa was an inventor. When he was young, he mainly invented serious things, but now that he was older, he mainly invented funny things. Frankie's favorite was the dancing potato.

Grandpa sat and did some inventing,
while Frankie lay on the floor looking for
scary pictures in a book of ancient tales.

Then Grandpa looked at his watch and
noticed that it was already 4:00.

"Where's Grandma?" he wondered.

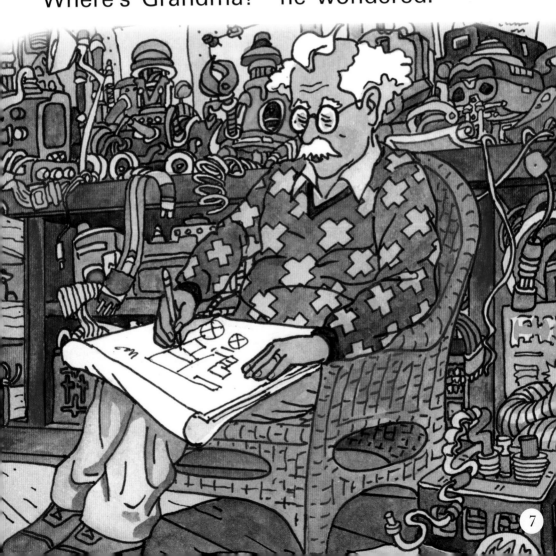

There was no sign of Grandma, Worrier, or the little old car anywhere.

"Where did she say she was going?" Grandpa asked.

"She said there was one more thing she had to do," answered Frankie. "Perhaps she's visiting a friend."

"I hope she didn't go to see Aziza Bibi in Zanzibar. But I have a feeling she did, and now we're going to have to get her," Grandpa said as he shook his head with worry.

Grandpa put his hands on a lever sticking out from the floor.

"Hold tight," he said as he pulled the lever and clicked it to the left.

There was a jolt, and the shed flew straight up into the air!

"Is this what you meant to happen?" asked Frankie, as the shed jumped over bumps and skipped over dips.

Grandpa nodded. Just as the shed reached the cliffs, it dropped—SLOSH—into the sea.

Frankie looked out the window. "It floats!" he said.

"I should hope so because I built this thing to last," Grandpa replied.

Frankie made a sail from a picnic tablecloth. Then with the wind behind them they glided onward.

It wasn't long before they reached Zanzibar, where they landed in between two fishing boats, scraping against the beach.

Grandpa and Frankie jumped onto the warm sand and noticed the smell of cinnamon in the air.

"That's where Grandma's friend lives," said Grandpa, pointing to a house with a carved door.

Aziza Bibi gave Frankie and Grandpa a warm welcome but said that she hadn't seen Grandma in weeks.

"I wonder where Grandma could be," Grandpa wondered aloud.

"Perhaps she took Worrier for a walk," suggested Frankie.

"You know where she likes to take Worrier for a walk!" Aziza Bibi added with a smile.

"Yep! I bet she went to Siberia," said Grandpa, "and we're going to have to get her."

They said good-bye to Aziza Bibi and went back to the shed.

"Hold on tight," Grandpa said, putting his hands tightly on the lever, pushing it, and clicking it to the right.

There was a thud as skis came out beneath the shed, and there was a clunk as propellers started whirling. Then they were off, jumping the waves.

"How did you come up with this invention?" asked Frankie.

Grandpa shrugged as he replied, "If you can invent a dancing potato, a shed like this is no problem."

The farther they went, the colder it got, and before long they reached Siberia.

"GRANDMA!" called Frankie as the shed slid to a stop in the white snow between several silver birch trees.

There was no reply as Frankie stuck his head out the shed door.

"Perhaps she decided to go shopping," suggested Frankie.

"Maybe you're right," agreed Grandpa.

"You know where she likes to go shopping," said Frankie.

"Yes, she loves shopping at the Chor Bazaar in Mumbai," stated Grandpa. "I have got a feeling she went to Mumbai," said Grandpa, "and we're going to have to get her."

"Hold on tight," Grandpa said as he pulled on the lever and clicked it up.

A small hatch flew open in the roof, and a large balloon came out and filled with a WHOOOOSH of hot air. Moments later, the shed was floating high up into the sky.

It wasn't long before they reached the market in Mumbai. Below them a crowd was swirling around stalls of carpets, bowls, shirts, bracelets, and cushions, but there was no sign of Grandma.

Grandpa seemed upset as he asked, "Where in the world could she be?"

That's when Frankie exclaimed, "Grandma said she was going to find some passion fruits for passion fruit cookies!"

"That might explain it!" exclaimed Grandpa. "Now where would she find passion fruits?"

"A tropical forest," Grandpa whispered to himself.

"Maybe the Amazon rain forest!" added Frankie.

"Yes!" exclaimed Grandpa. "I have a feeling that's where she went . . ."

"And we're going to have to get her," added Frankie.

"Do you want to fly us there, Frankie?" asked Grandpa.

"I'll try," agreed Frankie as he put his hands on the lever.

As Frankie pushed the lever and clicked it to the left, he exclaimed, "Hold on tight!"

There was a crackling sound from beneath the shed, and an inflatable rubber cushion came out. The balloon was sucked back into the roof, and the jet engines hissed from under the door. Now the shed was a hovercraft of sorts.

Off they sped through the clouds, and it wasn't long before they were looking down at the warm, green treetops of the Amazon rain forest. There was a sweet smell of flowers and leaves. Tree crickets chirped and snakes lay on the branches.

Off in the distance, Frankie spotted
Grandma's little old car. It was in the
top branches of a tree, and there were
Grandma and Worrier sitting in the car.

"GRANDMA!" shouted Frankie.

"FRANKIE, YOU FOUND US," Grandma
called back.

Monkeys went away squawking as the rubber cushion came to rest softly on the tops of the trees.

Frankie and Grandpa stepped on the trees and headed toward Grandma.

"Did you come all this way to find some passion fruits for your cookies, Grandma?" asked Frankie.

Grandma nodded and gave them both a big hug.

"This tree is full of them," Grandma said. "But would you believe the car wouldn't start?"

Grandpa looked at the sky and said, "It'll be dark soon. We need to get the car into the shed and head home."

They managed to roll the car into the shed. Then Grandma said, "Full speed home!"

"Grab the lever, Frankie." Grandpa nodded toward it and said, "Pull it toward you, then click it down."

Frankie put his hands on the lever and shouted, "Hold on tight!" Then he pulled the lever and clicked it down.

The jet engines hissed, the balloon
whooshed open, the skis dropped out
with a thud, and the propellers whirled.
Frankie helped put up the sail as well.
Soon they were headed home at double
speed.

It was dark by they time they reached
the ocean.

"When we get home we'll have our
passion fruit cookies and milk," said
Grandma.

While they flew home, Grandpa read the paper, and Frankie watched Grandma as she made the passion fruit cookie mix.

"Grandma," he said after a while, "how did your little old car end up on the top of a tree in the middle of the Amazon rain forest?"

"It's easy when you've got rocket boosters on your little old car," said Grandma with a laugh.

Grandpa looked up from his paper and said, "I told you those rocket boosters of yours needed to be fixed."